THE LAST YEARS OF
NORTH EAST
STEAM

PETER TUFFREY

GREAT NORTHERN

ACKNOWLEDGEMENTS

In compiling this book I am grateful for the assistance received from the following people: Ben Brooksbank, Doug Brown, David Burrill, David Clay, Peter Crangle, David Dippie, David Dunn, Peter Jary, David Joy, Hugh Parkin, Bill Reed.

Gratitude should also be expressed to my son Tristram for his general help and encouragement throughout the course of the project.

PHOTOGRAPHS

Every effort has been made to gain permission to use the photographs in this book. If you feel you have not been contacted please let me know: petertuffrey@rocketmail.com.

INFORMATION

I have taken reasonable steps to verify the accuracy of the information in this book but it may contain errors or omissions. Any information that may be of assistance to rectify any problems will be gratefully received. Please contact me by email: petertuffrey@rocketmail.com – or in writing: Peter Tuffrey, 8 Wrightson Avenue, Warmsworth, Doncaster, South Yorkshire, DN4 9QL.

Great Northern Books
PO Box 1380, Bradford, BD5 5FB
www.greatnorthernbooks.co.uk

© Peter Tuffrey 2018

ISBN: 978-1-912101-91-7

Design and layout: David Burrill

CIP Data
A catalogue for this book is available from the British Library
Printed & bound in India

INTRODUCTION

The railways have always been purveyed as an indispensable mover of people. Publicity departments of the 'Big Four' railway companies went to great lengths to entice passengers to use trains such as the 'Flying Scotsman', 'Coronation Scot', the 'Cheltenham Flyer' and 'Golden Arrow' to reach their destinations, emphasising luxury and speed. Such thinking was aided by the public's natural attraction to express passenger locomotives, which were often large, powerful, immaculately presented and bestowed with an imaginative name.

As with many areas, this is only a small portion of the reality. The railways, in the main, have always been reliant on freight traffic to generate revenue levels that made the operation sustainable and were unobtainable from passenger services. The London & North Eastern Railway (formed after the Grouping of 1923) is a particular example of this. Encompassing several areas of heavy industry over the inherited territories the company was threatened with collapse during the Depression when coal and steel traffic shrank to very low levels, but both recovered before the war.

Similarly, the network of lines in the North East of England reflected the dominance of freight and mineral traffic with the proliferation of coal mines, steel works, docks, etc. The area had been associated with railways from the early 17th century in the form of wagonways that carried coal from mines to the important rivers in the region. These systems were an important base for the next step in the development of railways. The weight of goods moved and timescale for this was limited by the capacity of the horses used, but the development of the steam engine attracted the colliery companies to test the new technology. One interested party was George Stephenson of Killingworth Colliery who developed several locomotives and his initial work culminated with the planning and building of the Hetton Colliery Railway in 1822.

With Stephenson's knowledge of railways and steam engines, he was approached to plan the Stockton & Darlington Railway and later to provide engines for use on the line. On 27th September 1825 the undertaking became the first public railway to use locomotives operated by steam power. From the beginning, the carriage of coal was the priority and passenger traffic was initially left to a third party before the S&DR took over in the 1830s.

The movement of people between Darlington and Newcastle was only achieved through the use of several sections of different companies' routes. There were no links between the inland population centres as the lines invariably went to the docks on the rivers. North of the Tyne the situation was different and the Newcastle & Berwick Railway beat the objections of Earl Grey to forge a link between not only the two places, but the eastern side of the country.

During the 1830s and 1840s railway companies sprang up at a fantastic rate, but, as in other industries, a few rose above the rest, which were enveloped. By the late 1840s three were dominating the area: York, Newcastle & Berwick; York & North Midland; Leeds Northern. At the start of the new decade the merger of the trio was carried out, forming the North Eastern Railway.

By the start of the First World War, the NER was one of the most successful railway companies in Britain, operating around 2,000 miles of track and carrying 60 million passengers. But this number is overshadowed by the colliery traffic which amounted to 52.5 million tons moved; nearly 19 million tons was sent to the ports, many of which were operated by the NER. Scores of other products were also sent to and from the industrial areas around the Rivers Tyne, Wear, Tees, etc.

At Grouping in 1923 the London & North Eastern Railway inherited the NER, but also received several other companies, the fortunes of which were quite different. The Depression years were not kind to the company and the North East was particularly affected, but business improved just before the Second World War. Great pressure was placed on the network during the conflict and maintenance and improvements were neglected.

British Railways was formed in 1948 and the North Eastern Region was formed out of the LNER's North Eastern Area, which consisted of much of the NER network. By now the success of the NER could only be dreamed of. Passenger and freight traffic steadily declined, despite attempts to improve services and cut those which had previously been supported by profits accumulated from mineral trains. The Modernisation Plan of 1955 and the subsequent amendments failed to revitalise the railways and the end result was not just the loss of steam locomotives, stations and routes, but a whole way of life for several generations.

Thankfully, the post-war boom in camera ownership has allowed the last decade or so of steam to be captured by a dedicated band of photographers for posterity. The North Eastern Region (here focussed on the area north of Darlington to Alnwick) was a particularly interesting area given the variety of locomotives to be seen at work.

The position of both the LNER and BR meant that neither concern was capable of large-scale replacement of pre-Grouping stock and NER locomotives were still at work up to the end of steam. T.W. Worsdell Class C (J21) 0-6-0s built between 1886 and 1895 could still be found up to the early 1960s, whilst W. Worsdell's P1 and P3 (J25 and J27) 0-6-0s developed in the early 20th century similarly survived until the final years of steam. Sir Vincent Raven was well-represented by his T2 (Q6) Class 0-8-0 which was a familiar sight on coal trains. The design was inspired by Worsdell's T and T1 0-8-0s and incorporated the use of piston valves — a new feature at the time — but a larger boiler with a superheater (also a novelty) was fitted to the new engines. Seventy were erected at Darlington Works between 1913 and 1919, with a further fifty purchased from Armstrong Whitworth between 1919-1921. Subsequently, the class could be found at many of the major freight depots across the North East, with the numbers allocated varying over their service life. The first withdrawal did not take place until the early 1960s and a large number were still at work until September 1967; the last engine condemned — no. 63344 — is seen in this collection close to that date at Washington.

Raven gave way to H.N. Gresley at Grouping and the latter's designs slowly began to permeate the area. Perhaps the first LNER class to establish itself was the A1 Pacifics (later A3), which would prove superior to Raven's hastily designed examples, as ten were sent to Gateshead along with another five to Heaton in 1924/1925. The numbers at these sheds would slightly increase over the years to work the principal expresses to Edinburgh and King's Cross, etc.

With the introduction of the 'Silver Jubilee' streamline train Gateshead received one of the new A4s to act as a standby for the other three in case of failure, but the shed would receive more from the general service batch to work expresses and Heaton would acquire an example. Later, the A4s were concentrated at three sheds, one of which was Gateshead and eight were put on the roster to work expresses. No. 60001 *Sir Ronald Matthews*, no. 60002 *Sir Murrough Wilson* and no. 60019 *Bittern* appear here at Gateshead, Durham and Sunderland; no. 60002 has the ignominy of hauling a ballast train past Forfar Street, Sunderland.

As large numbers of 0-6-0s were in service Gresley's J39 Class was not desperately required in the North East, but a good portion eventually found their way there due to the versatility of the class, being equally at ease on goods/mineral trains as excursion traffic. The J39s were withdrawn quite quickly in the late 1950s/early 1960s after being displaced from their normal areas. Several reached Alnmouth to work from there before being condemned and this is recorded here, as is the scrapping of a pair at Darlington Works.

After initially missing out on Gresley's V1, the North East received a sizeable quantity of engines, as well as the new V3s when they appeared. The locomotives were dispersed quite widely and were used on local services mainly, but also some further afield, such as trains to Carlisle. Both types are represented in this selection.

Gresley was succeeded by Edward Thompson, who introduced several classes during his relatively brief tenure before retirement. The most numerous was the B1 4-6-0 which fulfilled the intended workhorse role for many years. A number of the class members are included; several are those named after Antelope. One of the rarer Thompson classes to be seen in the North East was the O1 2-8-0s which were more closely associated with the Woodford express freights. Just five were allocated to Tyne Dock shed for the iron ore service and, if not heading, could be seen assisting these heavy trains, which were loaded from the iron ore carrying ships berthed at Tyne Dock, up the adverse gradients to Consett Steel Works.

The last Chief Mechanical Engineer of the LNER was A.H. Peppercorn and his A1 Pacifics became a familiar sight running up and down the East Coast Main Line with the principal expresses of the day. Also, the class was used on freight trains and several instances of this have been captured and included here, particularly at Sunderland Portobello Lane goods yard. Equally as visible were the K1 Class 2-6-0s, which were Peppercorn's development of the Thompson K4 rebuild based on the B1, and introduced to replace J39s on some of their duties.

During the war the War Department introduced a robust 2-8-0 (the 'Austerity') to work at home and abroad during the conflict. Large numbers were built and many were subsequently purchased by the LNER and BR at modest fees to replace older engines still working on the freight traffic, thus negating the expense of new construction. The class were not very glamorous, constantly appearing dishevelled and worn out, but appealed to photographers who did not discriminate against them in favour of an engine with a name. Similarly, the BR Standard Class 9F 2-10-0 caught the eye of many, especially with dramatic displays hauling the heavy iron ore traffic on the Tyne Dock-Consett service, for which ten were dedicated and distinguished through the fitting of Westinghouse air pumps on the right-hand side to operate the ore wagons' hopper doors.

Whilst the main line railways were of interest to some, others were equally enchanted by the many industrial locomotives employed by the various collieries, docks and steel works in the area. The National Coal Board had a sizable fleet of 0-6-0STs and a number from Ashington, Easington, Lambton, Philadelphia and Wearmouth Collieries are displayed here. Representing the docks are a number of Tyne Improvement Commission steeds and 0-4-0STs used at the wharves at Stockton. Similar types were employed at Consett Steel Works and Jarrow Metal Industries, where the crews are seen happily posing for the camera.

The end of steam in the North East came towards the end of 1967, signalling the start of the final decline of the railways and industry in the area. The attempts by BR to modernise and streamline were unfortunately unable to turn the tide against strengthening competition. Nevertheless, these images offer an interesting glimpse into the lost industrial landscape of the North East and effectively illustrate the proud history of the area.

Above ALNMOUTH STATION

No. 62021 was part of the K1 contingent at Alnmouth and is seen shunting at the south end of the station on 7th May 1966. Picture by John Boyes courtesy J.W. Armstrong Trust.

Below ALNMOUTH - WOODEN GATE SIDINGS

National Coal Board 0-6-0ST locomotive no. 46 shunts coal wagons at Wooden Gate sidings, just south of Alnmouth. Picture by John Boyes courtesy J.W. Armstrong Trust.

Above ALNMOUTH - SHILBOTTLE COLLIERY
Another view of NCB 0-6-0ST locomotive no. 46, but in this instance the location is Shilbottle Colliery, which was a short distance to the south west of Alnmouth. Picture by John Boyes courtesy J.W. Armstrong Trust.

Below ALNMOUTH VIADUCT
Thompson B1 Class 4-6-0 no. 61354 passes over the viaduct spanning the River Aln to the north of Alnmouth on 12th March 1966. Picture by John Boyes courtesy J.W. Armstrong Trust.

Above ALNMOUTH STATION
Peppercorn K1 2-6-0 no. 62025 was one of several class members allocated to Alnmouth shed during the latter days of steam. These engines were used on the local service to Alnwick, as well as to Newcastle, and on short-distance goods trains. No. 62025 was built by the North British Locomotive Company in August 1949 and was in service until April 1967. Here, the engine is seen running tender-first towards the Alnwick branch during September 1964. Picture by Bill Reed.

Opposite above ALNMOUTH STATION
Peppercorn A1 Class Pacific no. 60121 *Silurian* was completed at Doncaster just before Christmas 1948 and was initially allocated to York shed. Interestingly, the locomotive would be based there until condemned in early October 1965, being one of only a very small number of A1s at just one depot during their careers. No. 60121 — named in May 1950 — has been pictured at Alnmouth station with a down express during September 1964. Photograph by Bill Reed.

Opposite below ALNMOUTH STATION
This scene was also captured in September 1964 and shows Gresley V2 Class 2-6-2 no. 60982 with an up local service; standing opposite is Peppercorn K1 2-6-0 no. 62025. No. 60982 was erected at Darlington Works in June 1944 as the penultimate member of the class, which had been introduced eight years earlier and would number 184 members. The engine was based in the North East Area — from new until condemned during October 1964 — at only two sheds, York and Darlington, but only brief periods were spent at the latter. Picture by Bill Reed.

Above ALNWICK - WHITTLE COLLIERY

Located a short distance to the south of Alnwick, Whittle Colliery was operational by 1920 and worked the Shilbottle seam until closed in 1987. NCB 0-6-0ST no. 51 is seen here working from the colliery to the connection with the main line south of Warkworth. Picture by John Boyes courtesy J.W. Armstrong Trust.

Below ALNWICK

Peppercorn K1 Class 2-6-0 no. 62011 is seen at Alnwick station on 12th March 1966 with the 16.32 service to Alnmouth. Picture by John Boyes courtesy J.W. Armstrong Trust.

Above ALNMOUTH SHED

Gresley J39 Class 0-6-0 no. 64814 spent the last six months in service at Alnmouth and is pictured outside the shed on 11th June 1962, which was two months after arrival. Picture by Dave Tyreman courtesy J.W. Armstrong Trust.

Below ALNWICK STATION

K1 no. 62011 takes on water at Alnwick station as a DMU arrives with the 10.15 from Alnmouth on 12th March 1966. Photograph by John Boyes courtesy J.W. Armstrong Trust.

ALNWICK

Two views taken at Alnwick during mid-1965 featuring branch favourite, K1 no. 62025. Above, the engine awaits departure with a two-coach train to Alnmouth on 13th May 1965. Below, in mid-August, no. 62025 approaches the station with a train consisting of two passenger carriages and a parcels van. Both photographs by Bill Reed.

Above ALNWICK STATION
K1 no. 62011 comes away from the stock forming an Alnmouth to Alnwick service and moves to the other end of the train for the 12.30 return on 12th March 1966. Services would cease in just under two years' time after eighty years. Photograph by John Boyes courtesy J.W. Armstrong Trust.

Below ANNFIELD PLAIN
BR Standard Class 9F 2-10-0 no. 92062 helps at the rear of a standard train of nine ore wagons at Annfield Plain on the Tyne Dock-Consett line; other classes (O1s and Q7s) used on the traffic were restricted to eight wagons. Picture by Arthur Ives courtesy J.W. Armstrong Trust.

Above ANNFIELD PLAIN

Another BR Standard Class 9F 2-10-0 — no. 92064 — heads one of the frequent iron ore trains to Consett Steel Works at Annfield Plain; assisting is a BR Type 4 (Class 40) diesel. Picture by Arthur Ives courtesy J.W. Armstrong Trust.

Below ANNFIELD PLAIN

Raven Q6 0-8-0 no. 63381 takes on water at Annfield Plain on 22nd April 1966; the engine was withdrawn at the end of the year. Picture by Bill Wright.

Above ASHINGTON

J27 Class 0-6-0 no. 65861 is in charge of a train of empty coal hoppers at Ashington on 31st October 1966. Erected at Darlington in December 1921, the locomotive was in service to May 1967. Picture by Bill Wright.

Below ASHINGTON COLLIERY

View to the locomotive shed at Ashington Colliery on 10th April 1969. Many of the engines are stored on the left. Picture by Dave Tyreman courtesy J.W. Armstrong Trust.

ANNFIELD PLAIN

Two Raven Q6 Class 0-8-0s work a Consett-Jarrow oil train through Annfield Plain during April 1963. Leading is no. 63431 (built May 1920, withdrawn August 1967) and assisting at the rear is no. 63379 (completed in June 1917, condemned September 1966). The former was allocated to Tyne Dock, while the latter was a Consett engine. Photograph by P.J. Robinson.

Above ASHINGTON COLLIERY
NCB no. 40 working at Ashington Colliery on 7th August 1969. Picture by K. Gregory courtesy J.W. Armstrong Trust.

Below ASHINGTON COLLIERY
NCB no. 38 and no. 11, captured at Ashington Colliery in 1955. Picture by Derek Charlton courtesy J.W. Armstrong Trust.

Above ASHINGTON COLLIERY

Established in 1867, Ashington Colliery had a number of locomotives on hand to help with the daily tasks, two (no. 29 and no. 31) being seen. Picture by Dave Tyreman courtesy J.W. Armstrong Trust.

Below BILLINGHAM

View west from Billingham's original station to Wolviston Road bridge on 12th April 1966. Ex-War Department 'Austerity' 2-8-0 no. 90434 is seen moving on to the slow line with a coal train. Photograph by Geoff Warnes.

Above BILLINGHAM

Ivatt Class 4MT 2-6-0 no. 43056 approaches Billingham station from the east — passing over Station Road crossing — on 12th April 1966. The engine was West Hartlepool-allocated at the time and would be in traffic until the end of the year. Photograph by Geoff Warnes.

Below BILLINGHAM STATION

View east at Billingham station on 12th April 1966 as K1 no. 62007 waits for the road. The station was closed in late 1966 and replaced by a modern facility, which was located to the east; the footbridge and signal box survived the demolition of the station and still stand. Picture by Geoff Warnes.

Above BILLINGHAM
Raven Class Q6 no. 63387 travels towards Billingham station with a train of plate wagons from Stockton Malleable Iron Works to West Hartlepool on 31st August 1967. Photograph by John Boyes courtesy J.W. Armstrong Trust.

Below BISHOP AUCKLAND STATION
Bishop Auckland station was just one of the stops on the Stephenson Locomotive Society's 'Three Dales' railtour, undertaken on 20th May 1967; K1 no. 62005 was the sole steam locomotive used. Photograph by John Boyes courtesy J.W. Armstrong Trust.

Above BISHOP AUCKLAND STATION

Fairburn 4P 2-6-4T no. 42085 waits for parcels to be loaded at Bishop Auckland station on 12th August 1965. After withdrawal in October 1967 the engine was one of two class members preserved, both currently being based at the Lakeside and Haverthwaite Railway. Picture by Dave Tyreman courtesy J.W. Armstrong Trust.

Below BISHOP AUCKLAND STATION

Accommodated at the Crook platform, Bishop Auckland station, on 17th May 1963 is Stanier 4P Class 2-6-4T no. 42639. Photograph by R. Goad courtesy J.W. Armstrong Trust.

Above BISHOP AUCKLAND STATION

Another ex-London, Midland & Scottish Railway 2-6-4T has been engaged on the Crook service. Fairburn 4P no. 42194 was originally based in Scotland and remained there until late 1964. By 24th February 1965 Darlington had received the engine and withdrawal from there occurred in August. Photograph by R. Goad courtesy J.W. Armstrong Trust.

Below BISHOP AUCKLAND STATION

View south east from the Durham line platform to Bishop Auckland East signal box, which controlled the junction for this route and that to Crook. Picture by John Pedelty courtesy J.W. Armstrong Trust.

Above BISHOP AUCKLAND
Raven Q6 no. 63398 has been pictured to the east of Bishop Auckland with a short train of flat wagons on 28th December 1963. Photograph by R. Goad courtesy J.W. Armstrong Trust.

Below BISHOP AUCKLAND
The lines from Durham and the goods yard were controlled by the impressive Bishop Auckland North signal box, seen here on 8th March 1968. Picture by John Boyes courtesy J.W. Armstrong Trust.

Above BISHOP AUCKLAND STATION
On a cold and snowy 2nd March 1965, Fairburn 4P no. 42194 simmers at the head of a train sheltered under the covering for the Crook platform at Bishop Auckland station. This was the only place on the route still served, but these services would also cease during the month. Photograph by R. Goad courtesy J.W. Armstrong Trust.

Below BISHOP AUCKLAND STATION
Worsdell J21 0-6-0 no. 65078 had the honour of leading the last passenger train to Wearhead on 27th June 1953. Picture by B.W.L. Brooksbank.

Above BLAYDON SHED

Reid 'Scott' Class 4-4-0 no. 62432 *Quentin Durward* stands in the yard at Blaydon shed before working back to Hawick with the 16.30 service from Newcastle. Photograph by K.H. Cockerill courtesy J.W. Armstrong Trust.

Below BLAYDON SHED

Peppercorn A1 Pacific no. 60539 *Bronzino* at Blaydon shed, with Raven Q6 no. 63394 on the right, 24th May 1961. The latter was allocated, whilst the former was a Heaton resident. Picture by D.J. Dippie.

Above BLAYDON STATION

View west from the footbridge over the Redheugh branch to Blaydon station on 10th May 1965. Sweeping away to the right behind the signal box is the line from Carlisle to Newcastle Central station; this section has since been closed. Blaydon station remains open, but has been rebuilt. Photograph by B.W.L. Brooksbank.

Opposite above BLAYDON SHED

Worsdell J27 Class no. 65802 was erected at Darlington Works in June 1908 as the third locomotive in the order for ten to be completed. The engine is pictured at Blaydon shed around mid-1957 when allocated to Percy Main depot, which was a long-term residence of no. 65802. Withdrawal from Blyth North shed occurred in August 1966. Photograph by Bill Reed.

Opposite below BOWESFIELD

'Austerity' 2-8-0 no. 90434 heads north through Bowesfield, south of Stockton, with a train of empties bound for West Hartlepool on 5th January 1967. Picture by John Boyes courtesy J.W. Armstrong Trust.

Above CAMBOIS
Worsdell J27 Class no. 65874 approaches with a loaded coal train at Cambois on 11th Jan 1965. Photograph by Geoff Warnes.

Below CHESTER-LE-STREET
K1 no. 62045 leads Type 4 (Class 45) diesel D129 over Chester-le-Street Viaduct. Picture by V. Wake courtesy J.W. Armstrong Trust.

Opposite above CHESTER-LE-STREET
Gresley A3 no. 60049 *Galtee More* at Chester-le-Street. Photograph by Malcolm Dunnett courtesy J.W. Armstrong Trust.

Opposite below CHESTER-LE-STREET STATION
Gresley V2 no. 60831 approaches Chester-le-Street station from the north. Picture by V. Wake courtesy J.W. Armstrong Trust.

Above CHESTER-LE-STREET STATION

Gresley A4 Class Pacific no. 60025 *Falcon* spent many years working from King's Cross shed and has been well turned out from there, with the highly burnished buffers shining here. The engine is at the head of a down express (with headboard reversed) at Chester-le-Street. Picture by Malcolm Dunnett courtesy J.W. Armstrong Trust.

Opposite above CHESTER-LE-STREET STATION

A.H. Peppercorn's A1 Pacific design was the culmination of the LNER's 30 years' experience with the type for express passenger duties. Yet, the locomotives were also suitable for heavy freight work given their ample reserve of power and were often called up for these tasks. No. 60124 *Kenilworth* is seen rushing through Chester-le-Street station with a train of oil tanks. Photograph by Malcolm Dunnett courtesy J.W. Armstrong Trust.

Opposite below CHESTER-LE-STREET

Worsdell J25 Class 0-6-0 no. 65728 waits in the goods yard line at Chester-le-Street station, whilst Raven Q6 Class 0-8-0 no. 63377 dramatically speeds northward with a train of loaded coal wagons. No. 65728 was built at Gateshead Works in December 1902 and was in service until April 1962 when withdrawn from Gateshead shed; most of the BR period had been spent working from Borough Gardens depot, Gateshead. No. 63377 was erected at Darlington during June 1917 and was in traffic until November 1966; the locomotive was also based at Borough Gardens during the 1950s. Picture by Malcolm Dunnett courtesy J.W. Armstrong Trust.

CONSETT STEEL WORKS

Two weary-looking workers pose with 0-4-0ST B No. 17 at Consett Steel Works on 17th August 1956, whilst the locomotive similarly stands for the camera outside the imposing offices. Both pictures by Derek Charlton courtesy J.W. Armstrong Trust.

Above CHOPWELL WOODS

NCB no. 48 speeds through Chopwell Woods on 13th June 1958. Photograph by Derek Charlton courtesy J.W. Armstrong Trust.

Below CONSETT

Raven Q6 no. 63398 reverses under Park Road bridge, Consett, during 1965. The locomotive was built at Darlington Works in December 1918 and was in service until October 1965 when withdrawn from Tyne Dock after 16 months there. Picture by Ernie Brack.

Above DARLINGTON SHED
Gresley A3 no. 60058 *Blair Athol* on Darlington shed's turntable. Photograph by Bill Reed.

Opposite DARLINGTON BANK TOP STATION
Peppercorn A2 no. 60533 *Happy Knight* at Darlington Bank Top station. Picture by Bill Reed.

Below DARLINGTON
Robinson A5 Class 4-6-2 no. 69842 stands withdrawn at Darlington during mid-1959 and awaits scrapping at the works. Construction was carried out by Hawthorn Leslie in March 1926. Picture by Bill Reed.

Above DARLINGTON WORKS
J94 Class no. 68007 is seen working in Darlington Works' yard. Photograph by Bill Reed.

Below DARLINGTON WORKS
Worsdell J21 Class 0-6-0 no. 65033 stands in the works yard at Darlington on 19th September 1965 awaiting preservation; withdrawal had occurred in April 1962. Picture by Geoff Warnes.

Above DARLINGTON WORKS
Stanier Class 5 4-6-0 no. 44734 under repair at Darlington Works on 26th September 1964. Photograph by J. Archer courtesy J.W. Armstrong Trust.

Below DARLINGTON WORKS
Two of Gresley's J39 Class 0-6-0s — no. 64704 and no. 64860 — meet their fate at Darlington Works' scrapyard on 9th July 1963. Picture by D.J. Dippie.

Above **DARLINGTON WORKS**

Despite being late in the day for steam — 30th October 1965 — repairs are still being undertaken at Darlington Works and the Erecting Shop is full of engines trying to beat the executioner. Nearest is Worsdell J27 Class 0-6-0 no. 65880 (withdrawn June 1967), behind three WD 'Austerity' tenders are the frames of K1 2-6-0 no. 62004 (condemned December 1966) and WD 'Austerity' no. 90503 (sent for scrap January 1967). Photograph by A.R. Thompson courtesy J.W. Armstrong Trust.

Opposite below **DARLINGTON SHED**

Constructed at Doncaster Works in May 1937, Gresley A4 Class Pacific no. 60010 *Dominion of Canada* spent most of the next 25 years working from King's Cross shed. The last two elapsed at Aberdeen Ferryhill before being condemned in May 1965 while awaiting repair at Darlington. No. 60010 was then stored at Darlington shed until August 1966 when taken to Crewe for restoration before being presented to the Canadian Railroad Historical Association. *Dominion of Canada* is seen languishing at the shed on 15th November 1965. Picture by D.J. Dippie.

Above DARLINGTON SHED
Worsdell J27 Class no. 65815 has been a recent visitor to Darlington Works for overhaul and is at Darlington shed for running in before returning home to Blyth North shed on 9th July 1963. The locomotive had been built by the North British Locomotive Company in May 1908 and was condemned in November 1966. Photograph by D.J. Dippie.

Above DARLINGTON
Worsdell J27 Class no. 65784 is seen at Darlington attached to a train of loaded coal wagons. Photograph by Bill Reed.

Below DARLINGTON WORKS
The cutters have been hard at work on Worsdell J72 Class 0-6-0T no. 68708 in Darlington Works' scrapyard. The engine had been withdrawn from West Auckland in August 1961 after just under a year there. Photograph by C. Clayson.

Above DARLINGTON SHED
A relatively quiet scene outside Darlington shed on 19th July 1965. Facilities had been established on the site from at least 1866, but the building seen here was erected in 1940 by the LNER and had seven roads. Photograph by Bill Wright.

Below DARLINGTON SHED
No. 68047 was one of 75 0-6-0ST bought by the LNER from the WD in 1945/46. The engine was then engaged at Darlington until May 1965. Picture by Bill Reed.

Above DARLINGTON/COATHAM MUNDEVILLE
Heading an express freight at Coatham Mundeville, north of Darlington, on 9th July 1963 is Gresley V2 Class 2-6-2 no. 60974. Photograph by D.J. Dippie.

Below DARLINGTON SHED
No. 60036 *Colombo* was constructed at Doncaster in July 1934 as an A3 Class engine. Working from Gateshead initially, *Colombo* would have several allocations to North East sheds before withdrawal in November 1964, the last being Darlington from December 1963. Picture by D.J. Dippie.

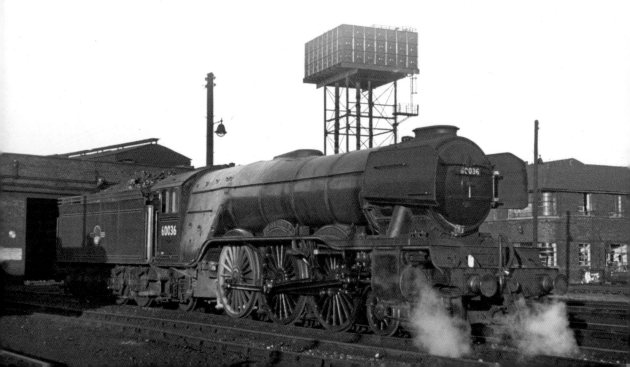

Above DARLINGTON
Several locomotives are seen out of service at Darlington. Leading is Worsdell J72 Class no. 69006 and behind is Worsdell J21 Class no. 65117. Photograph by Bill Reed.

Below DARLINGTON SHED
Thompson B1 no. 61274 is serviced in the shed yard at Darlington; the locomotive resided there between September 1955 and June 1959. Picture by Bill Reed.

Above DURHAM STATION

BR Standard Class 'Britannia' Pacific no. 70023 *Venus* makes a rare appearance in the north east at Durham station on 15th July 1961, coming off the viaduct with a down express. The locomotive was allocated to Cardiff Canton shed at this time and regular duties would have normally kept *Venus* on the lines to Paddington, Bristol, Shrewsbury and Salisbury. In the south end bay platform on the left is no. 67688. Picture by D.J. Dippie.

Below DURHAM STATION

Following completion at Darlington in January 1932, Gresley J39 Class no. 64833 worked for the next twenty years from sheds in the eastern counties. For three years before withdrawal in November 1962, no. 64833 was allocated to Sunderland shed and has travelled from there to Durham station on 15th July 1961. The engine is seen ready to return with a 'Durham Miners' Gala' special. Photograph by D.J. Dippie.

Above DURHAM STATION

Durham station was opened by the North Eastern Railway in 1857, but was later rebuilt in the early 1870s. Pulling into the platform is a down express for Newcastle headed by Gresley A4 Pacific no. 60002 *Sir Murrough Wilson* on 15th July 1961. Picture by D.J. Dippie.

Below DURHAM STATION

A variety of coal wagons forming an up train are hauled through Durham station on 28th May 1960 by Peppercorn K1 no. 62062. The engine was one of seventy K1s erected by the NBLC between 1949/1950 and entered service in January 1950 to Darlington. No. 62062 had just returned there following three years at York. Picture by D.J. Dippie.

Above DURHAM STATION

Stanier Class 5 no. 44930 speeds north through Durham station with a parcels service for Newcastle. The class rarely operated in the North East and, as the locomotive was a long-term resident at Blackpool shed, this sight was quite unusual. Photograph by Arthur Ives courtesy J.W. Armstrong Trust.

Below DURHAM STATION

Gresley V3 Class 2-6-2T no. 67690 stands on the north-west side of Durham station, which is now part of the car park. Photograph by Arthur Ives courtesy J.W. Armstrong Trust.

Above DURHAM
Darlington's no. 60916 runs south light engine on 2nd March 1963 a short distance south of Durham station. Picture by Howard Forster.

Below DURHAM STATION
One of the few English Peppercorn A2 Pacifics — no. 60538 *Velocity* — gets away from Durham with a northbound express on 16th July 1960. Photograph by D.J. Dippie.

Above EAST HETTON COLLIERY

An NCB 0-4-0ST appears to have been abandoned at East Hetton Colliery, south east of Durham, on 17th November 1968. The pit was sunk in 1836 and was operational for just short of 150 years. Photograph by John Boyes courtesy J.W. Armstrong Trust.

Below EAST HETTON COLLIERY

Another view of the 0-4-0ST at East Hetton Colliery; note the works plate has been removed. Photograph by John Boyes courtesy J.W. Armstrong Trust.

Above EASINGTON COLLIERY
NCB 0-6-0ST no. 24 is seen at Easington Colliery on 22nd April 1959. The first coal was extracted in 1910 and production continued until 1993. Picture L.G. Charlton Collection courtesy J.W. Armstrong Trust.

Below EASINGTON
With Easington Colliery in the background, Gresley J39 0-6-0 no. 64812 heads south with a train of passenger stock. Photograph by Malcolm Dunnett courtesy J.W. Armstrong Trust.

Above EASINGTON COLLIERY

Neglected Raven Q6 no. 63450 prepares to leave Easington Colliery with a train of coal wagons during July 1965. Picture by Ernie Brack.

Below EASINGTON COLLIERY

In a similar state is classmate no. 63395 which is also seen at Easington, but on 4th February 1967. Photograph by John Boyes courtesy J.W. Armstrong Trust.

Above GATESHEAD SHED

Raven Q6 no. 63342 passes Gateshead shed with a train of mineral wagons in the late 1950s/early 1960s. In the background there is activity involving the depot's Cowans Sheldon breakdown crane. Picture by Howard Forster.

Below GATESHEAD SHED

Worsdell N10 Class 0-6-2T no. 69109 outside Gateshead shed; the engine was a long-term resident. Constructed at Darlington in April 1903, no. 69109 would survive until April 1962. Picture by Bill Reed.

GATESHEAD SHED

Gresley A3 Class Pacific no. 60092 *Fairway* had three allocations to Gateshead shed. The final period lasted from June 1963 to October 1964 when condemned. Picture by Chris Campbell.

Above GATESHEAD SHED
In over 26½ years Gresley A4 Class Pacific no. 60001 *Sir Ronald Matthews* had only one allocation, which was to Gateshead. The engine was withdrawn in October 1964 and was scrapped in the north east at Hughes, Bolckow, Blyth. Photograph by Bill Reed.

Below GATESHEAD SHED
The usual high standard of cleanliness for A4 Class Pacifics based at King's Cross has been allowed to lapse and no. 60025 *Falcon* appears decidedly dishevelled at Gateshead in March 1963. King's Cross closed a short time later and after four months at Peterborough, no. 60025 was scrapped. Photograph by Howard Forster.

Above GATESHEAD SHED

An illustrious group of locomotives are serviced at Gateshead shed on 11th April 1964: A3 no. 60054 *Prince of Wales*; A1 no. 60119 *Patrick Stirling*; A3 no. 60106 *Flying Fox*; A4 no. 60002 *Sir Murrough Wilson*. Picture by Chris Campbell.

Below GATESHEAD SHED

A3 no. 60045 *Lemberg* at Gateshead. Ten years were spent at Doncaster following completion in late 1927, but the next 27 years saw the engine either at Heaton, Darlington or Gateshead. Picture by Chris Campbell.

Above GATESHEAD WORKS
Gresley V3 no. 67690 is in the midst of a light repair at Gateshead Works on 30th May 1964; five months would be added to the engine's life. Picture by Ian Falcus.

Below GATESHEAD
Gresley V2 no. 60929 makes a dramatic display of reversing from Gateshead shed to Newcastle station on 1st May 1965. Photograph by Malcolm Dunnett courtesy J.W. Armstrong Trust.

Above GATESHEAD SHED
Thompson B1 no. 61014 *Oribi* on the north side of Gateshead shed with a view across the Tyne to Newcastle.
Photograph by Howard Forster.

Below GATESHEAD SHED
Two of the recent additions to Worsdell's J72 Class — no. 69005 and 69028 — are seen at Gateshead shed. Picture by
Howard Forster.

Above HARTBURN
'Austerity' no. 90434 heads south through Hartburn, near Stockton-on-Tees, with the 11.55 West Hartlepool to York coal train on 20th September 1966. Photograph by John Boyes courtesy J.W. Armstrong Trust.

Below HARTBURN
A4 no. 60004 *William Whitelaw* turns at Hartburn after working the first leg of the Blyth & Tyne Railtour from Leeds to Eaglescliffe on 19th September 1965. Picture by John Boyes courtesy J.W. Armstrong Trust.

Above HARTBURN

V2 no. 60964 passes the junction for the Middlesbrough line at Hartburn with a train bound for Colchester on 27th April 1957; B1 no. 61018 *Gnu* travels in the opposite direction. Picture by John Phillips from the Alan Bowman Collection courtesy J.W. Armstrong Trust.

Below HARTLEPOOL STATION

Raven H1/A8 Class 4-6-2T no. 69888 at Hartlepool station. Open from 1880, the station replaced an earlier facility built in 1841 for the Stockton & Hartlepool Railway. Picture D.R. Dunn Collection.

Above HEATON

A1 Pacific no. 60126 *Sir Vincent Raven* travels south through Heaton with an empty stock train for Newcastle on 24th May 1961. The engine was allocated to the local shed, but would soon move on to York and was condemned there in 1965. Picture by D.J. Dippie.

Below HEATON

View from Heaton Road to North View, Heaton, as Worsdell J27 no. 65825 travels towards Newcastle with a fish train from Tynemouth on 24th September 1962. Photograph courtesy J.W. Armstrong Trust.

Above HEATON SHED

Thompson A2/3 Pacific no. 60517 *Ocean Swell* has the fire grate cleaned at Heaton shed on 24th May 1961. In September the engine was one of several Pacifics to be moved on from the depot as more diesels came into operation. Picture by D.J. Dippie.

Below HEATON SHED

Worsdell J27 Class no. 65886 at Heaton Shed during the late 1950s. The locomotive was withdrawn in August 1959 from North Blyth shed after 36 years in traffic. Picture by Bill Reed.

Above HEXHAM

Worsdell J71 0-6-0T no. 68278 is on light duties at Hexham goods yard shunting a solitary coal wagon. Photograph by Ken Taylor.

Below HEXHAM STATION

B1 no. 61219 stands at Hexham station on 2nd August 1951. The engine had been in works earlier in the year, yet still has BR lettering and would not receive the emblem until the next works visit the following year. Picture by L.G. Charlton courtesy J.W. Armstrong Trust.

Above HEXHAM SHED

Hexham shed (seen in 1958) was only 13 years old when closed by BR in mid-1959; two earlier sheds had been destroyed by fire. Picture by K. Groundwater courtesy J.W. Armstrong Trust.

Below HEXHAM

The safety of the Border Counties Bridge was one of the reasons for the closure of the line between Riccarton and Hexham on 13th October 1956. BR Standard Class 3 2-6-0 no. 77011 is seen passing over the bridge on the last day. Picture by W.I.O. Moffat from M. Halbert Collection.

Above HEXHAM STATION

View north east to Hexham station with Gresley V1 no. 67658 at the platform. Photograph by E.E. Smith from M. Halbert Collection.

Below HEXHAM

No. 77014 approaches Hexham with a branch service on 2nd July 1956. Picture by W.I.O. Moffat from M. Halbert Collection.

Above HEXHAM STATION

Thompson B1 no. 61014 *Oribi* speeds east with an express. For eight years after construction in 1946 the engine resided at Gateshead and would continue to be associated with the North East until condemned in December 1966. Photograph by J.W. Armstrong courtesy J.W. Armstrong Trust.

Below JARROW

Armstrong Whitworth (Metal Industries) No. 2 at the Jarrow site on 7th April 1965. Picture L.G. Charlton Collection courtesy J.W. Armstrong Trust.

Above JARROW
0-4-0ST locomotive B no. 38 at work in Jarrow on 2nd February 1955. Photograph L.G. Charlton Collection courtesy J.W. Armstrong Trust.

Below JARROW
Palmer's Shipbuilding & Iron Co. was founded in 1852 and expanded to cover 100 acres by 1900. But in the Depression the company struggled and collapsed in 1933, being sold off in parts. Jarrow Metal Industries was formed and traded until 1953 when taken over by Armstrong Whitworth. 0-4-0ST no. 1 is seen on 22nd June 1950. Photograph L.G. Charlton Collection courtesy J.W. Armstrong Trust.

Above LAMBTON
NCB no. 29 keeps the coke moving in spite of frigid conditions at Lambton Coke Works. Photograph by Frank Bell courtesy J.W. Armstrong Trust.

Below LAMBTON STAITHES
A brakeman hitches a ride with NCB no. 47 at Lambton Staithes during June 1955. Photograph by Derek Charlton courtesy J.W. Armstrong Trust.

Above LAMBTON COLLIERY
NCB no. 5 at Lambton Colliery. Picture by Frank Bell courtesy J.W. Armstrong Trust.

Below LAMBTON STAITHES
NCB no. 5 wears a green livery at Lambton Staithes in June 1955. Photograph by Derek Charlton courtesy J.W. Armstrong Trust.

LINTON

A local miners' train from Linton Colliery to Ashington is headed by NCB no. 31 during 1964; note the NCB lettering on the carriages. Linton Colliery — to the east of the ECML between Pegswood and Widdrington — was sunk in the mid-1890s and worked several seams until closure in 1968. Picture by P.J. Robinson.

MIDDLESBROUGH

Three ex-London, Midland & Scottish Railway locomotives await scrapping at Cargo Fleet, Middlesbrough, on 18th October 1968. All — no. 44780, no. 44845 and no. 44818 — are of W.A. Stanier's Class 5 4-6-0 design and were condemned at Newton Heath shed in June. Photograph by John Boyes courtesy J.W. Armstrong Trust.

Above MIDDLESBROUGH STATION

Fairburn 4P Class 2-6-4T brings empty stock into Middlesbrough station on 5th August 1965. Photograph by R. Goad courtesy J.W. Armstrong Trust.

Below MIDDLESBROUGH CARGO FLEET

0-4-0ST no. 6 shunts wagons at Cochrane's Steel Works, Cargo Fleet, on 27th December 1967. Photograph by John Boyes courtesy J.W. Armstrong Trust.

Above MIDDLESBROUGH SHED
Gresley V1 no. 67677, Gresley J39 no. 64756 and Ivatt 4MT no. 43074 have gathered round the turntable at Middlesbrough shed on 13th June 1954. Picture by B.W.L. Brooksbank.

Below MIDDLESBROUGH SHED
The odd sight of J72 Class no. 68740 with a bike attached has been captured at Middlesbrough shed on 13th June 1954. Picture by B.W.L. Brooksbank.

Above MIDDLESBROUGH - DORMAN LONG
No. 43 at Dorman Long's Britannia Works (on the eastern bank of the Tees), 16th June 1957. Picture by C.W. Allen courtesy J.W. Armstrong Trust.

Below MIDDLESBROUGH
Worsdell J71 no. 68312 is seen with a train carrying metal pipes at Middlesbrough Dock on 5th January 1959. Picture by John Mallon.

MONKSEATON

A1 no. 60121 at Monkseaton, 1964. Several stations have served the area and the present facility dates from 1915, being designed by William Bell, noted architect for the NER. Photograph by Les Ferguson courtesy J.W. Armstrong Trust.

Above MORPETH

Worsdell J27 no. 65869 comes off the down goods loop at Morpeth on 22nd September 1966. Photograph by John Boyes courtesy J.W. Armstrong Trust.

Below MORPETH STATION

The last passenger train from Morpeth to Rothbury, 15th September 1952, headed by no. 67341. Picture from M. Halbert Collection.

Above MORPETH - PEGSWOOD COLLIERY

Two miles east of Morpeth, Pegswood Colliery was only a year away from closure when NCB no. 8 was seen there during late March 1968. Picture by John Boyes courtesy J.W. Armstrong Trust.

Below MORPETH - PEGSWOOD COLLIERY

NCB no. 8 shunts wagons for loading at Pegswood Colliery on 25th March 1968. Photograph by John Boyes courtesy J.W. Armstrong Trust.

MORPETH
NCB no. 46 shunts tipper coal wagons at Morpeth. Photograph by John Boyes courtesy J.W. Armstrong Trust.

Above MORPETH

A1 no. 60127 *Wilson Worsdell* hauls an express passenger train through Morpeth, 1st August 1964. The station serving the town was opened by the Newcastle & Berwick Railway in March 1847 and is still operational for the local population; thankfully the baronial-style station building survives intact. Picture by Howard Forster.

Below MORPETH

K1 no. 62050 at Morpeth with a coal train in June 1966. Picture by Ernie Brack.

Above MORPETH

A Gateshead Gresley V2 no. 60962 moves light engine through Morpeth on 1st August 1964. The engine would be withdrawn just over a year later from the shed. Picture by Howard Forster.

Below MORPETH

A1 Pacific no. 60116 *Hal o' the Wynd* was another locomotive with a working life that was based from sheds in the North East. Picture by Howard Forster.

Above NEWBIGGIN STATION
Gresley V3 no. 67651 is at the head of a local service from Newbiggin station in June 1956. Photograph from M. Halbert Collection.

Below NEWBIGGIN STATION
A local service to Newbiggin has arrived at the station behind Worsdell G5 Class 0-4-4T no. 67323. Photograph from D.R. Dunn Collection.

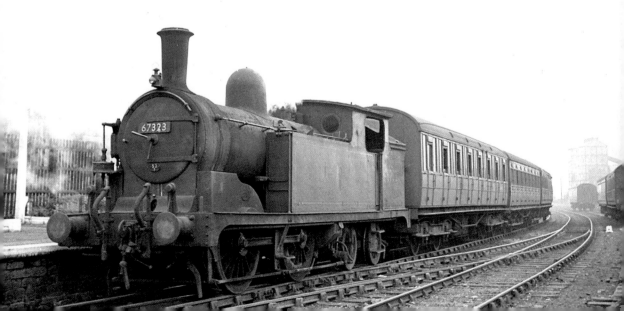

NEWBIGGIN STATION

The crew and guard of this train happily pose for a picture at Newbiggin station. The locomotive is Worsdell G5 no. 67341. Picture from D.R. Dunn Collection.

Above NEWBIGGIN COLLIERY
NCB no. 1 *Teddy* at Newbiggin Colliery on 6th June 1964. Photograph by I.H. Hodgson courtesy J.W. Armstrong Trust.

Below NEWBIGGIN STATION
Newbiggin station was opened in early 1872 by the Blyth & Tyne Railway and survived until November 1964. The colliery is seen on the right and this closed in 1967. Picture by Roy Stevens.

NEWCASTLE STATION

Worsdell J72 no. 68736 was one of two engines decorated in NER green for shunting at Newcastle and York stations. The locomotive is seen at the former on 26th May 1962. Photograph by Howard Forster.

Above NEWCASTLE STATION
A standard liveried Worsdell J72 no. 68693 is seen shunting (the van visible is designated fruit) at Newcastle station. The locomotive was a long-term Gateshead resident. Picture by Bill Reed.

Below NEWCASTLE STATION
Gresley A3 no. 60086 *Gainsborough* gets away from Newcastle station with the up 'Queen of Scots' Pullman on 10th February 1962. Photograph by D.J. Dippie.

Above NEWCASTLE STATION
Gresley V1 no. 67641 was close to being withdrawn when pictured at Newcastle station on 26th May 1962. In October the engine was sent for scrap after 27 years in traffic. Photograph by Howard Forster.

Below NEWCASTLE STATION
Thompson A2/3 no. 60522 *Straight Deal* reverses on to stock from either Gateshead or Heaton at Newcastle station during June 1962 and would soon depart for Edinburgh Waverley. Photograph by Howard Forster.

Above NEWCASTLE STATION

V3 2-6-2T no. 67651 makes a water stop at Newcastle station on 24th May 1961 whilst marshalling vans at the east end. The engine was built at Doncaster in January 1936 with V1 specifications, but later became V3 in May 1956. Photograph by D.J. Dippie.

Below NEWCASTLE STATION

A total of 82 V1 Class engines were erected at Doncaster between 1930 and 1939, followed by 10 V3s. The difference between the two was the boiler, with the latter having a higher pressure, and this was subsequently fitted to 59 V1s — no. 67653 was a recipient in September 1954. The locomotive is seen at the west end of Newcastle station on 1st August 1960. Picture by D.J. Dippie.

Above **NEWCASTLE STATION**
Thompson B1 no. 61199 was built by the NBLC in June 1947 and lasted in service until January 1967. During June 1962, the engine is seen going on to a northbound train at Newcastle. Photograph by Howard Forster.

Below **NEWCASTLE STATION**
Although initially allocated to Heaton, A4 no. 60003 *Andrew K. McCosh* was subsequently based in the south. King's Cross-allocated when captured at Newcastle on 12th August 1961, the engine is reversing on to a train for Edinburgh. Photograph by Howard Forster.

Above NEWCASTLE STATION

Raven Q6 no. 63385 takes the avoiding lines on the southern side of Newcastle station on 4th November 1960 with this train of coal wagons. The locomotive was allocated to Blaydon at this time and would be condemned after a short spell at Sunderland. Photograph by D.J. Dippie.

Below NEWCASTLE STATION

A4 no. 60022 *Mallard* simmers in the cold, snowy conditions at Newcastle station on 19th January 1963. The engine was only three months away from being withdrawn at this time and was preserved. Picture by Howard Forster.

Above NEWCASTLE STATION
At Newcastle on 2nd March 1963 is Aberdeen-based A2 no. 60525 *A.H. Peppercorn*. Picture by Howard Forster.

Below NEWCASTLE STATION
A1 no. 60161 *North British* is ready to leave Newcastle with a down express during the early 1960s. Photograph by Howard Forster.

Above **NORTH BLYTH**
Raven Q6 no. 63354 began life in May 1913, emerging from Darlington Works as no. 1278. The engine later received no. 3354 in April 1946 and BR's '6' prefix in June 1948. No. 63354 was a Blyth North locomotive when seen near the town at the head of this up train on 11th January 1965. Picture by Geoff Warnes.

Below **NORTH BLYTH SHED**
Worsdell J27 no. 65802 at North Blyth shed on 18th June 1965. Picture by Bill Reed.

NORTON EAST JUNCTION

WD 'Austerity' no. 90434 takes Norton East Junction from the West Hartlepool line to the Leeds Northern line on 7th December 1965. The engine would take this coal train on the latter line as far as Northallerton and then take the ECML to York, which was the destination. Picture by John Boyes courtesy J.W. Armstrong Trust.

Above NORTH SEATON

North Seaton station was open from 1859 until 1964. Passing through with a coal train from Ashington Colliery to Cambois/North Blyth power station on 2nd November 1966 is Worsdell J27 no. 65804. Picture by Bill Wright.

Below NORTON EAST JUNCTION

Travelling towards West Hartlepool past Norton East Junction is WD 'Austerity' no. 90011 on 13th May 1966. The dolomite train had originated at Thrislington a short distance away. Picture by John Boyes courtesy J.W. Armstrong Trust.

PELAW JUNCTION

In June 1959 Raven Q6 no. 63377 was transferred from Borough Gardens shed to Blaydon. The engine is seen during the month at Pelaw Junction, which saw lines to Jarrow and Washington diverge north and south respectively from the line to Sunderland. Photograph by Bill Reed.

Above PELAW JUNCTION
In June 1959 the switchover to electric signalling is in evidence at Pelaw Junction; by the end of the following year a new signal box opened there replacing several in the area. Q6 no. 63371 passes by with a brake van. Picture by Bill Reed.

Below PELAW JUNCTION
Heading towards Pelaw Junction on the Washington branch line (with Follonsby Colliery in the background) is Q6 no. 63429 on 12th June 1967. The engine was condemned at the start of July. Photograph by Trevor Ermel.

Above PHILADELPHIA COLLIERY

NCB 0-6-2T no. 29 (left) and no. 5 (right) at Philadelphia Colliery, 5½ miles south west of Sunderland. Picture by Kevin Hudspith courtesy J.W. Armstrong Trust.

Below PENSHAW

NCB no. 42 moves coal wagons at Penshaw, north of Philadelphia and south east of Washington. Photograph by I.S. Carr courtesy J.W. Armstrong Trust.

Above PHILADELPHIA COLLIERY
NCB no. 51 working hard at Philadelphia Colliery. Picture by I.S. Carr courtesy J.W. Armstrong Trust.

Below PHILADELPHIA
View north at Philadelphia as NCB no. 63 approaches the crossing; the Penshaw monument is visible on the left.
Picture by John Boyes courtesy J.W. Armstrong Trust.

Above PHILADELPHIA COLLIERY

NCB no. 7 stands next to the coaling stage at Philadelphia Colliery while NCB no. 63 waits in the shadow of the headgear. Picture by John Boyes courtesy J.W. Armstrong Trust.

Below PERCY MAIN

In August 1965 Worsdell J27 no. 65812 passes by with a mineral train and 20-ton brake van at Percy Main. Until recently the engine had been a long-term resident at the local engine shed, then taking a berth at Blyth North. Picture by Bill Reed.

Above SHILDON

View from the south-east end of Shildon station as Peppercorn K1 no. 62008 approaches with a freight train on 1st April 1965; in the distance are the large Shildon Sidings. Picture by R. Goad courtesy J.W. Armstrong Trust.

Below SHILDON

Spout Lane bridge (seen above) provides the vantage point for this scene taken on 7th April 1965 looking north west to Shildon station. Another K1 (no. 62064) is seen and is passing a diesel shunter, which is perhaps moving wagons for attention in Shildon Works. Photograph by R. Goad courtesy J.W. Armstrong Trust.

Above SHILDON
Q6 no. 63351 is seen on the Bishop Auckland line just north of Shildon station with a train of empty coal wagons on 9th November 1963. Picture by R. Goad courtesy J.W. Armstrong Trust.

Below SHILDON STATION
View south to Shildon station as B1 no. 61176 approaches with empty stock on 15th June 1963. Picture by R. Goad courtesy J.W. Armstrong Trust.

Above SHILDON STATION

A local service pauses at Shildon station on 3rd April 1965. Leading the train is Fairburn 4P Class no. 42194 which was erected at Derby Works in April 1948 and in service until August 1965. Mainly based in Scotland, Gateshead and Darlington were the engine's last allocations. Photograph by R. Goad courtesy J.W. Armstrong Trust.

Below SHILDON STATION

Parcels are loaded on to this local train at Shildon on 27th August 1965 as no. 42213 waits for the off. Photograph by R. Goad courtesy J.W. Armstrong Trust.

Above SLEEKBURN
The area between the River Blyth and River Wansbeck was heavily industrialised with no less than six collieries standing amongst other concerns. J27 no. 65879 is seen at Sleekburn with a train of coal wagons on 11th January 1965. Photograph by Geoff Warnes.

Opposite SOUTH BLYTH SHED
J27 no. 65822 outside South Blyth shed. Picture by Bill Reed.

Below SOUTH BLYTH SHED
South Blyth shed was mainly for mineral engines, but there were also some 0-4-4Ts stabled there for local passenger trains. The former is represented here in the form of J27 no. 65862. The shed closed to steam in May 1967. Picture by Bill Reed.

Above SOUTH BLYTH SHED

Several sheds were established on the south side of the River Blyth, to the west of the station. The most enduring was erected in 1880 by the NER for over £2,000. Soon after the three tracks provided were deemed inadequate and the space was doubled by providing a similar structure on the northern side in 1894. The ramped coal stage built at this time was sited to the east on the north side of the lines to the station. Worsdell J27 no. 65861 receives fuel from the stage on 1st November 1966. Photograph by Bill Wright.

Opposite above STOCKTON

A short distance to the south of Stockton station, Ivatt 4MT 2-6-0 no. 43128 approaches with a train of loaded coal wagons on 19th June 1965. The engine was constructed at Horwich Works in October 1951 and briefly sent to Hull Dairycoates depot before being moved on to Heaton. By the time this image was captured, no. 43128 had reached West Hartlepool by way of Alston and Kirkby Stephen and had been there since mid-1956. Looking the worse for wear (the last general repair had been completed at Horwich in October 1962), the locomotive was condemned in July. Photograph by Dave Tyreman courtesy J.W. Armstrong Trust.

Opposite below STOCKTON

View south from the footbridge seen in the picture of no. 43128 as Peppercorn K1 no. 62001 moves an ore train on 23 May 1966; on the right is Moor Steel & Iron Works. The locomotive still had a year left in traffic and had just moved from Darlington to West Hartlepool. No. 62001 would have two months at York from February 1967 until condemned. Photograph by John Boyes courtesy J.W. Armstrong Trust.

STOCKTON

K1 no. 62045 is seen with a Tees Yard to West Hartlepool mineral train at Stockton on 21st September 1966. Photograph by John Boyes courtesy J.W. Armstrong Trust.

Above STOCKTON STATION

A busy scene on the western side of Stockton station as Peppercorn K1 no. 62044 takes on water, whilst BR Type Three (later Class 37) D6776 passes by with a mineral train (note the brake tender) on 19th April 1967. Picture by John Boyes courtesy J.W. Armstrong Trust.

Below STOCKTON STATION

Ivatt 4MT no. 43057 takes on water at Stockton station before heading to Tees Yard, while a DMU is at the platform on 2nd September 1966. Picture by John Boyes courtesy J.W. Armstrong Trust.

STOCKTON NORTH SHORE

Ivatt 4MT no. 43100 hauls a mixed freight train through the heavily industrialised North Shore area of Stockton on 13th September 1966. Picture by John Boyes courtesy J.W. Armstrong Trust.

Above **STOCKTON NORTH SHORE**
The signalman of North Shore signal box, Stockton, poses for the camera on 15th September 1966. Photograph by John Boyes courtesy J.W. Armstrong Trust.

Below **STOCKTON - CORPORATION WHARF**
A Robert Stephenson & Hawthorns 0-4-0ST is engaged at Stockton Corporation Wharf on 13th August 1965. Photograph by John Boyes courtesy J.W. Armstrong Trust.

STOCKTON NORTH SHORE

WD 'Austerity' no. 90014 passes Stockton North Shore signal box with the 11.55 West Hartlepool to York coal train on 16th September 1966. Picture by John Boyes courtesy J.W. Armstrong Trust.

Above STOCKTON - TYNE TEES WHARF

Tyne Tees Wharf, Stockton, (on the west bank, north of Bridge Road — the Cleveland Flour Mill on the opposite bank is prominent) is where running repairs are being carried out on this diesel shunter.   Picture by John Boyes courtesy J.W. Armstrong Trust.

Below STOCKTON NORTH SHORE

No. 90434 with coal empties on 13th September 1966. Erected at Vulcan Foundry in January 1944, the engine was allocated in the North East from 1947 with periods spent at Heaton, Newport, Thornaby, Tyne Dock and West Hartlepool. Picture by John Boyes courtesy J.W. Armstrong Trust.

Above STOCKTON NORTH SHORE
No. 62045 heads north to West Hartlepool with a coal train on 21st September 1966 as another approaches.
Photograph by John Boyes courtesy J.W. Armstrong Trust.

Below STOCKTON STATION
No. 62045 is seen again at Stockton, but in this instance is passing Bishopton signal box with the 11.35 West Hartlepool to York loaded coal train on 8th August 1966. Picture by John Boyes courtesy J.W. Armstrong Trust.

Above STOCKTON NORTH SHORE
No. 90434 is seen again (from page 109). The engine still had nine months left in traffic before being withdrawn from West Hartlepool. Picture by John Boyes courtesy J.W. Armstrong Trust.

Below STOCKTON - TYNE TEES WHARF
Robert Stephenson & Hawthorns 0-4-0ST no. 6 in between duties at Tyne Tees Wharf, Stockton. Picture by John Boyes courtesy J.W. Armstrong Trust.

STOCKTON STATION

Gresley A3 Pacific no. 60084 *Trigo* adds some glamour amidst the procession of freight locomotives running through Stockton. On 10th June 1957 the engine heads an up relief express for Manchester. Picture by John Phillips from the Alan Bowman Collection courtesy J.W. Armstrong Trust.

Above STOCKTON

A line of locomotives — mostly comprising Gresley V1/V3s — await the end at T.J. Thompson & Son's scrapyard, Stockton, on 13th March 1965. The two at the head of the line are identifiable as no. 67638 and no. 67643, both of which had been condemned at Gateshead in November 1964. Picture by R. Goad courtesy J.W. Armstrong Trust.

Below STOCKTON STATION

Darlington-allocated Fairburn 4P Class no. 42085 takes on water at the north end of Stockton station on 6th February 1965. A further two years would elapse before withdrawal from Normanton. Photograph by R. Goad courtesy J.W. Armstrong Trust.

STOCKTON

Thompson B1 no. 61034 *Chiru* travels south tender-first with a train of empty stock for Redcar on 10th June 1957. Allocated to Stockton at this time (1949-1959), the engine would leave for Thornaby. Picture by John Phillips from the Alan Bowman Collection courtesy J.W. Armstrong Trust.

Above SUNDERLAND SHED
Only one locomotive from Raven's Q6 Class of 120 survived into preservation. No. 63395 was purchased in late 1967 and the locomotive is seen here at Sunderland shed in September. Photograph by Bill Reed.

Below SUNDERLAND SHED
Q6 no. 63441 at Sunderland shed on 23rd May 1963; the engine was withdrawn from there at the end of the year after 43 years' service. Picture by D.J. Dippie.

Above SUNDERLAND - PORTOBELLO LANE

A1 no. 60138 *Boswell* with goods vans in Sunderland Portobello Lane goods yard on 12th April 1962. Photograph by D.J. Dippie.

Opposite SUNDERLAND SHED

Judging from the scorching on the smokebox door and surrounding area, cleaning inside has not been a task favoured by the firemen of Q6 no. 63437 — a sizable deposit of ash lays in front of the locomotive, which is seen at Sunderland shed on 23rd April 1966. The locomotive was condemned at the depot during June 1967. Photograph by Bill Wright.

Below SUNDERLAND - PORTOBELLO LANE

V2 no. 60982 at Portobello Lane goods yard, Newcastle Road, on 13th April 1962. This area is presently the site of the Stadium of Light Metro station. Picture by D.J. Dippie.

SUNDERLAND - PORTOBELLO LANE

A1 no. 60150 *Willbrook* departs Portobello Lane
goods yard in the early evening of 19th June 1962
with a pick-up goods train destined for
Dringhouses, York. Picture by D.J. Dippie.

SUNDERLAND - PORTOBELLO LANE

V2 no. 60967 is seen marshalling two containers at Portobello Lane during June 1962. The locomotive is preparing to take a pick-up goods train to Dringhouses; the engine was allocated to York at the time. Picture by D.J. Dippie.

SUNDERLAND - PORTOBELLO LANE

Three people supervise the coupling of this train to Gresley A3 no. 60060 *The Tetrarch* at Portobello Lane on 29th June 1962. Photograph by D.J. Dippie.

SUNDERLAND - MONKWEARMOUTH STATION

Two views of Gresley V3 no. 67651 heading the Royal Train at Monkwearmouth station, Sunderland, on 26th July 1963. The Duke of Edinburgh was using the carriages on his visit to Sunderland, where he called at Jobling & Co. Glass Works (famous for producing Pyrex), two shipyards and laid the foundation stone for the Royal Naval Association building on Roker Avenue. No. 67651 of Gateshead shed has been specially turned out for the occasion. Both Photographs by D.J. Dippie.

Above SUNDERLAND SHED
After the fire and smokebox had been cleaned at Sunderland shed J27 no. 65872 was ready to return to work. The depot had the engine on the roster for many years before withdrawal in January 1967. Photograph by Bill Reed.

Opposite SUNDERLAND SHED
Four J27s are seen inside the roundhouse at Sunderland shed. From left to right they are: no. 65879, no. 65882, no. 65855 and no. 65894. Only the second to last mentioned was not allocated to the depot under BR and was a resident at Blyth until withdrawn. Picture by I.S. Carr courtesy J.W. Armstrong Trust.

Below SUNDERLAND SHED
A pair of A8 Class 4-6-2Ts — no. 69883 and no. 69853 — are out of service at Sunderland shed. The latter was a long-term resident, but the former was only briefly allocated. Picture by Bill Reed.

Above SUNDERLAND STATION

A4 no. 60030 *Golden Fleece* leaves Sunderland station with the 12.06 to Colchester on 7th June 1962; on the left is V3 no. 67688 and a DMU. Picture by D.J. Dippie.

Below SUNDERLAND - PORTOBELLO LANE

A3 no. 60045 *Lemberg* reverses into Portobello Lane goods yard with vans forming the Dringhouses pick-up freight on 11th July 1963. The building being erected is the Excel bowling alley on Newcastle Road. Photograph by D.J. Dippie.

Above SUNDERLAND - FORFAR STREET
View south from Forfar Street, Sunderland, as A4 no. 60002 *Sir Murrough Wilson* approaches with a loaded ballast train on 17th May 1962. Photograph by D.J. Dippie.

Below SUNDERLAND STATION
A3 no. 60036 *Colombo* has charge of the 10.16 express from Newcastle to Liverpool which is three minutes late in departing from Sunderland station on 12th August 1960. Picture by D.J. Dippie.

Above SUNDERLAND - FORFAR STREET
Peterborough New England's V2 no. 60853 heads an express past Forfar Street, Sunderland, on 23rd July 1961.
Photograph by D.J. Dippie.

Below SUNDERLAND SHED
At Sunderland shed on 30th June 1961 is Thompson B1 no. 61038 *Blacktail*. The engine had recently arrived from
Gateshead and would stay for a year before leaving for Blaydon. Picture by D.J. Dippie.

Above SUNDERLAND - PORTOBELLO LANE

A Heaton V2 — no. 60904 — has travelled to Portobello Lane goods yard on 28th June 1961. The engine was withdrawn from Gateshead in July 1964. Photograph by D.J. Dippie.

Below SUNDERLAND - PORTOBELLO LANE

Shunting takes place at Portobello Lane goods yard on 14th June 1961 as B16/3 Class 4-6-0 no. 61454 moves a number of vans and containers. Picture by D.J. Dippie.

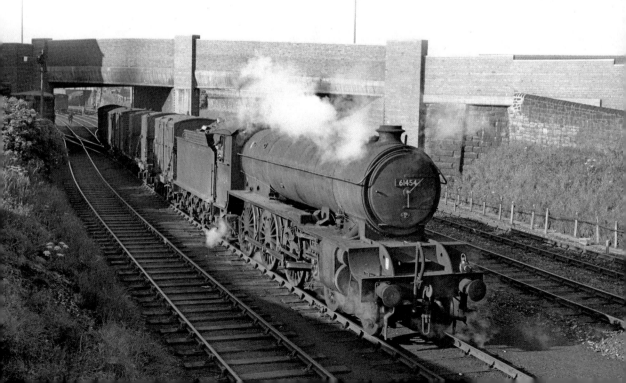

Above SUNDERLAND - FULWELL
Worsdell J25 Class 0-6-0 no. 65726 waits for the right of way at Fulwell (looking to Wearmouth Drive), north Sunderland, on 11th August 1960. The engine, which has a northbound coal train, was coming to the end of a year-long spell at Sunderland shed and would move on to Gateshead. Photograph by D.J. Dippie.

Below SUNDERLAND STATION
Gresley A3 no. 60085 *Manna* departs from the south end of Sunderland Central station with the 07.53 express to King's Cross on 26th July 1960. Picture by D.J. Dippie.

Above SUNDERLAND STATION

One A4 to spend many years in the North East was no. 60019 Bittern, which is seen here leaving Sunderland Central station on 26th July 1960. The engine is at the head of the 07.32 relief service — for the 07.53 seen opposite below — to King's Cross. Photograph by D.J. Dippie.

Below SUNDERLAND - PORTOBELLO LANE

York's A2/3 no. 60515 *Sun Stream* had six months left in traffic when photographed at Portobello Lane goods yard on 17th May 1962. Picture by D.J. Dippie.

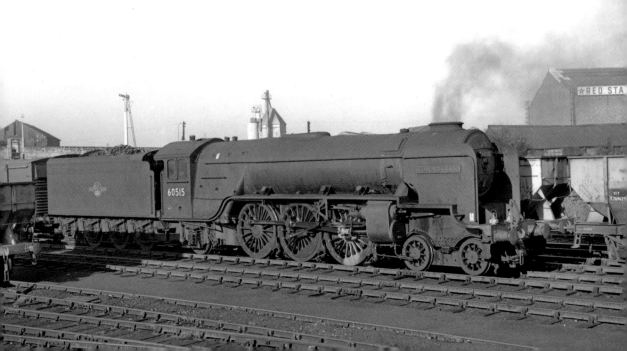

Above THORNABY STATION

Q6 no. 63397, with a loose coupled freight train, has been stopped by a signal at Thornaby station before entering Tees Yard on 17th April 1967. As a result the fireman has called the signalman to remind him of the train's presence in accordance with the rules. Picture by Bill Wright.

Below THORNABY STATION

Despite appearing to be travelling leisurely through Thornaby station with a train of mineral empties on 20th April 1961, Q6 no. 63388 was working at 'full throttle' according to the photographer which was perhaps due to the crew wishing to increase their mileage bonus for the day. Picture by B.W.L. Brooksbank.

Above TYNE COMMISSION QUAY
Work levels have dropped sufficiently for the driver of Tyne Improvement Commission 0-6-0ST no. 7 to put his feet up and keep warm. Picture by D.G. Charlton courtesy J.W. Armstrong Trust.

Below TYNE COMMISSION QUAY
TIC no. 9 is more gainfully employed shunting wagons at Tyne Commission Quay. Picture by D.G. Charlton courtesy J.W. Armstrong Trust.

Above TYNE COMMISSION QUAY
TIC 0-6-0ST no. 21 makes a fine display on 28th July 1954. Picture from L.G. Charlton Collection courtesy J.W. Armstrong Trust.

Opposite above TYNE COMMISSION QUAY STATION
A boat train has been brought into Tyne Commission Quay station, c. 1960 and Gresley V3 no. 67642 is ready to remove the empty stock. The locomotive was erected at Doncaster Works in July 1935 as a V1 Class engine and was subsequently converted to V3 in April 1960. At Nationalisation, no. 67642 was allocated to Heaton and at the end of 1957 moved on to Tweedmouth, only to return six months later. The locomotive did not move again until June 1964 when transferred to Gateshead and withdrawal from the depot took place a year later. Tyne Commission Quay station was a relatively recent addition to the area, being built in the late 1920s to replace an earlier facility, but was closed in mid-1970. Photograph by Eric Wilson courtesy J.W. Armstrong Trust.

Opposite below TYNE COMMISSION QUAY
For many centuries the Tyne has been an important point for the transportation of goods from the surrounding area. From the 17th century the most important commodity sent to the docks was coal which amassed great wealth for Newcastle. Yet, the river was allowed to deteriorate to the point where at low tide certain points were only covered by a few feet of water. This led to the formation of the Tyne Improvement Commission which consisted of various representatives from the local area and associated industries. Matters were soon improved as the river was dredged and new facilities provided, such as Albert Edward Dock — the site's grain warehouse being seen here in the background — Northumberland Dock, several piers and many staithes. There were extensive railway lines and sidings that were worked by a small army of locomotives, no. 1 being pictured on 25th March 1953. Photograph by L.G. Charlton courtesy J.W. Armstrong Trust.

TYNE DOCK

In 1962 a Type 4 diesel locomotive was tested on the Tyne Dock-Consett service and found to be quite capable. This led to a gradual takeover from the 9Fs which was complete by the winter of 1966. To commemorate the end, BR Standard Class 9F no. 92063 was specially prepared to work 'The Tyne Docker' on 19th November 1966. The locomotive is seen here near Tyne Dock working hard and creating a fine display for passengers in the brake vans attached to the rear of the train. Picture by Chris Campbell.

Above TYNE DOCK SHED
9F no. 92064 is serviced at Tyne Dock shed, which was home between May 1956 and November 1966. Photograph by K.H. Cockerill courtesy J.W. Armstrong Trust.

Below TYNE DOCK - GREEN LANE JUNCTION
NCB 'B' Area 0-6-0ST no. 6 comes off the Harton line at Tyne Dock Green Lane Junction with a train of empty hoppers for Boldon Colliery on 21st April 1966. Picture by Bill Wright.

TYNE DOCK

9F no. 92063 is seen again working hard at Tyne Dock, in this instance with a mineral train bound for Consett. Picture courtesy J.W. Armstrong Trust.

Above WASHINGTON
Worsdell J21 no. 65099 had a career spanning 70 years from 1891-1961 and is seen here towards the end at Washington. Photograph by Frank Bell courtesy J.W. Armstrong Trust.

Below WASHINGTON
Red warning flags stop traffic on the Brady's Square/Railway Terrace crossing, Washington, as no. 63426 travels on the colliery branch, 14th June 1967. The engine was condemned a week later. Picture by K. Gregory courtesy J.W. Armstrong Trust.

Above WASHINGTON STATION

Two boys make an early start to prospective careers as engine cleaners, while a third is perhaps considering a superintendent position. They are humoured by the crew of Gresley V3 no. 67689, which stands at the head of a train at Washington station on 14th September 1956. The engine was Gateshead-allocated at this time and would be until December 1962; shortly after withdrawal occurred and no. 67689 was scrapped at Darlington. Photograph by I.S. Carr courtesy J.W. Armstrong Trust.

Above WASHINGTON
K1 no. 62060 had only two months left in traffic when seen at Washington during June 1967. Picture by K. Gregory courtesy J.W. Armstrong Trust.

Opposite below WASHINGTON
Washington 'F' Colliery (to the north west of the station) was founded in 1777 and produced coal until 1968. Here, an NCB locomotive from the pit is seen at the Village Lane Crossing. Photograph by V. Wake courtesy J.W. Armstrong Trust.

Below WASHINGTON 'F' COLLIERY
An NCB 0-6-0ST locomotive moves coal wagons under the dispenser at Washington 'F' Colliery. Photograph by V. Wake courtesy J.W. Armstrong Trust.

Above WASHINGTON
An old wooden coal wagon from Lambton Colliery intrudes upon this train of newer hoppers from Washington 'F' Colliery which is moved by an unidentified NCB 0-6-0ST past the coal drops; a road lorry appears overloaded. Picture by V. Wake courtesy J.W. Armstrong Trust.

Opposite above WASHINGTON
Apart from a four-year spell in West Yorkshire during the early 1960s (at Neville Hill and Normanton), Raven Q6 no. 63426 had strong links with sheds in the Teesside area. Working from Tyne Dock when seen acting as Washington Colliery pilot on 14th June 1967, the engine was condemned at the shed eight days later. Picture by K. Gregory courtesy J.W. Armstrong Trust.

Opposite below WASHINGTON STATION
A down local service has stopped at Washington station around 1948; the V3 locomotive at the head of the train — no. 7643 — has the LNER number and lettering on the tank side. BR no. 67643 from November 1948, the engine was allocated to Gateshead during this period and would later reside at Blaydon before withdrawal in April 1962. Photograph by W.A. Camwell courtesy J.W. Armstrong Trust.

Above **WASHINGTON**

Worsdell J21 0-6-0 no. 65039 began life from Gateshead Works in June 1889 as a compound locomotive but was later converted to simple expansion (with piston valves) in October 1910. Unlike other members of the extensive class, the engine was not superheated; further modification involved the brakes and Westinghouse equipment was fitted shortly after grouping, followed by vacuum apparatus in 1930 — no. 65039 originally had steam brakes. Allocated to Tyne Dock shed when seen here shunting at Washington Chemical Works, the locomotive was condemned at the shed in November 1958. Picture by S.C. Crook courtesy J.W. Armstrong Trust.

Opposite above **WASHINGTON STATION**

Heaton V3 no. 67691 has stopped at Washington station with a local service heading for Durham Miners' Gala on 19th July 1958. This event was established in the early 1870s and has continued up to the present time despite the coal mines in the area closing. No. 67691 was erected at Doncaster Works in April 1940 and was in traffic until November 1964. The engine moved from Heaton to Gateshead in mid-1963 and was condemned at the latter. Photograph by I.S. Carr courtesy J.W. Armstrong Trust.

Opposite below **WASHINGTON STATION**

Washington station was opened on 1st October 1850 as the second facility to serve the area following alterations to the original route between Ferryhill and Pelaw. This subsequently formed part of the main line between King's Cross and Edinburgh until a new route was taken to the west in the 1870s. Up to the early 20th century the station was quite busy, but passengers and services steadily declined until closed during early September 1963. With the industry in the area — Washington Chemical Works was off on the right — the station was a focal point for goods traffic. Worsdell J21 no. 65099 is seen at the south end of the station during the mid-1950s. Picture by W.R.E. Lewis courtesy J.W. Armstrong Trust.

Left WASHINGTON
The driver and fireman of no. 65099 pose for the camera; the engine was withdrawn in October 1961. Picture by W.R.E. Lewis courtesy J.W. Armstrong Trust.

Below WASHINGTON
Q6 no. 63358 on the unguarded crossing at Brady's Square, Washington. The locomotive was a mainstay at Borough Gardens shed during the 1950s, but for the last five years in traffic no. 63358 worked from Tyne Dock and was condemned there in March 1964. Picture by W.R.E. Lewis courtesy J.W. Armstrong Trust.

Above WASHINGTON

After a brief spell in the Midlands, 9F no. 92065 was allocated to Tyne Dock and would remain until condemned in April 1967. The engine is seen passing Washington Lane signal box. Photograph by I.S. Carr courtesy J.W. Armstrong Trust.

Below WASHINGTON

9F no. 92064 has a train of 56-ton bogie iron ore wagons, which were used exclusively for the Tyne Dock-Consett service, at Washington on 22nd April 1958. Picture by C. Campbell courtesy J.W. Armstrong Trust.

Above WASHINGTON

The Thompson O1 2-8-0 is well known for working the Annesley-Woodford freights, but five of the class were at Tyne Dock for the Consett trains until replaced by 9Fs. Here, no. 63856 is seen at Washington. Photograph courtesy J.W. Armstrong Trust.

Below WASHINGTON

J21 no. 65039 at work on the goods lines between Washington station and Washington Chemical Works on 17th July 1958. Photograph by W.R.E. Lewis courtesy J.W. Armstrong Trust.

Above WEARMOUTH COLLIERY

Wearmouth Colliery, Monkwearmouth, Sunderland, was established in the 1830s and continued production until 1993. NCB no. 2 works in the yard opposite Southwick Road on 19th April 1968. Photograph by Dave Tyreman courtesy J.W. Armstrong Trust.

Below WASHINGTON

Q6 no. 63344 heads south from Washington station with a train of mineral wagons on 14th June 1967. Picture by K. Gregory courtesy J.W. Armstrong Trust.

Above WEARMOUTH COLLIERY
NCB 0-6-0T *Jean* was employed at Wearmouth from 1909 until 1971 and is seen there on 3rd July 1956. Photograph by C.W. Allen courtesy J.W. Armstrong Trust.

Below WEARMOUTH COLLIERY
NCB 0-6-0ST no. 5 with NCB brake van at Wearmouth Colliery on 19th April 1968. Photograph by Dave Tyreman courtesy J.W. Armstrong Trust.

Above WESTOE LANE STATION

Westoe Lane station was opened by the South Shields, Marsden & Whitburn Colliery Railway in 1900, replacing an earlier facility named South Shields. The station mainly handled worker traffic to Whitburn Colliery, which was a large employer in the area, but this role ceased on 22nd November 1953 to increase line capacity for coal trains. The last train to run in daylight is seen here. Picture by Walter Dendy courtesy B.W.L. Brooksbank.

Below WHITBURN COLLIERY STATION

An NCB 0-6-0ST is at the head of the last train to Whitburn Colliery station on 22nd November 1953. Photograph by Walter Dendy courtesy B.W.L. Brooksbank.

WEST HARTLEPOOL

An unidentified WD Austerity 2-8-0 runs past Newburn
Junction signal box, West Hartlepool, on 16th June 1967.
Picture by John Boyes courtesy J.W. Armstrong Trust.

Above WEST HARTLEPOOL - CLIFF HOUSE SIDINGS

'Austerity' no. 90014 is seen in Cliff House Sidings, West Hartlepool, on 7th September 1967, with the old South Durham Iron & Steel Works in the background. Picture by John Boyes courtesy J.W. Armstrong Trust.

Below WEST HARTLEPOOL

No. 90478 leaves West Hartlepool steel works with a train of mineral wagons on 8th September 1967. Entering service from Vulcan Foundry in mid-1944, the engine worked in Nottinghamshire from the mid- to late 1940s, then transferring to Yorkshire. The last three months in traffic from June 1967 saw the engine in County Durham at West Hartlepool. Photograph by John Boyes courtesy J.W. Armstrong Trust.

WEST HARTLEPOOL - STRANTON
No. 90382 on a down empties train at Stranton,
West Hartlepool, on 13th June 1967. Photograph
by John Boyes courtesy J.W. Armstrong Trust.

Above WEST HARTLEPOOL SHED
The last home for Q6 no. 63407 was West Hartlepool shed and the engine is seen there shortly after withdrawal in early July 1967. Picture by John Boyes courtesy J.W. Armstrong Trust.

Below WEST HARTLEPOOL SHED
The yard at West Hartlepool shed is fully occupied on 27th November 1966: no. 90309; 63368; 63397; an unidentified 'Austerity'; a diesel shunter. Photograph by John Boyes courtesy J.W. Armstrong Trust.

Above WEST HARTLEPOOL SHED
The NER took over the Hartlepool West Harbour & Dock Company in the mid-1860s and found the engine stabling facilities to be inadequate, necessitating the erection of a new building. This was sited on land to the south of the station on the west side of the running lines, adjacent to Mainsforth Terrace. The new shed was opened in 1867 and had three roads; the centre lane contains 'Austerity' no. 90074 on 27th July 1967, with Q6 no. 63407 on the left and another 'Austerity', no. 90625, on the right. In spite of the dilapidated state of the roof, the facility remained open until September, but would later be torn down. Photograph by John Boyes courtesy J.W. Armstrong Trust.

Opposite WEST HARTLEPOOL
View south from Cliff House Road, West Hartlepool, on 20th July 1967. 'Austerity' no. 90677 is at the head of an up coal train passing the extensive steel works, which were founded in the 1860s as the West Hartlepool Steel & Iron Co., later the South Durham Steel & Iron Co. after several companies merged. On the left are Cliff House Sidings and in the foreground two wagons filled with timber acknowledge the other industry prominent in the area — saw mills. No. 90677 was a recent arrival in the area from Hull and would remain until condemned in September. The steel works has since been closed and the site cleared for housing. Photograph by John Boyes courtesy J.W. Armstrong Trust.

WEST HARTLEPOOL

Q6 no. 63387 passes Newburn Junction signal box on the way to collect the 13.00 train from West Hartlepool 'B' Yard to Tees Yard on 31st August 1967. Picture by John Boyes courtesy J.W. Armstrong Trust.

Above WEST HARTLEPOOL

'Austerity' no. 90687 is seen next to West Hartlepool's coal stage after leaving the shed on 31st August 1967. Picture by John Boyes courtesy J.W. Armstrong Trust.

Below WEST HARTLEPOOL

Ivatt Class 4MT no. 43015 was allocated to West Hartlepool for 12 years between 1955 and 1967, only being broken by a brief spell at Thornaby. The engine is at Newburn Junction (adjacent to the shed) on 14th June 1967. Picture by John Boyes courtesy J.W. Armstrong Trust.

WEST HARTLEPOOL SHED

A pair of roundhouses were built to supplement the straight shed at West Hartlepool during the early 1870s. Nestling inside one on 27th July 1962 is Q6 no. 63387 with an unidentified BR Class 04 diesel shunter. Photograph by John Boyes courtesy J.W. Armstrong Trust.

Above WOODBURN STATION
On the Wansbeck Railway line between Morpeth and Reedsmouth, Woodburn station was only open for freight from 1952 to 1966. Here, on 22nd September 1966, the weekly goods train from Morpeth makes a stop. Photograph by John Boyes courtesy J.W. Armstrong Trust.

Below WOODBURN
Worsdell J27 no. 65842 (also seen above) climbs out of Woodburn with the Morpeth goods. Picture by John Boyes courtesy J.W. Armstrong Trust.

BIBLIOGRAPHY

Bolger, Paul. *BR Steam Motive Power Depots: North Eastern Region*. 2009.

Griffiths, Roger and John Hooper. *The Directory of British Engine Sheds and Principal Locomotive Servicing Points: 2 North Midlands, Northern England and Scotland*. 2000.

Hoole, K. *A Regional History of the Railways of Great Britain Volume 4: The North East*. 1974.

Hoole, K. *North Eastern Locomotive Sheds*. 1972.

Hoole, K. *Rail Centres: Newcastle*. 2008.

Hooper, J. *The WD Austerity 2-8-0: The BR Record*. 2010.

Pike, S.N. *Mile by Mile on the LNER: King's Cross Edition*. 1951.

Quick, Michael. *Railway Passenger Stations in Great Britain: A Chronology*. 2009.

RCTS. *Locomotives of the LNER: Part 2A*. 1978.

RCTS. *Locomotives of the LNER: Part 2B*. 1975.

RCTS. *Locomotives of the LNER: Part 5*. 1984.

RCTS. *Locomotives of the LNER: Part 6A*. 1982.

RCTS. *Locomotives of the LNER: Part 6B*. 1991.

RCTS. *Locomotives of the LNER: Part 6C*. 1984.

RCTS. *Locomotives of the LNER: Part 7*. 1991.

RCTS. *Locomotives of the LNER: Part 8B*. 1971.

RCTS. *Locomotives of the LNER: Part 9A*. 1977.

RCTS. *British Railways Standard Steam Locomotives Volume 1*. 1994.

RCTS. *British Railways Standard Steam Locomotives Volume 4*. 2008.

Sixsmith, Ian. *The Book of the Ivatt 4MTs*. 2012.

Walmsley, Tony. *Shed by Shed Part Three: North Eastern*. 2010.

Yeadon, W.B. *Yeadon's Register of LNER Locomotives Volume One*. 2001.

Yeadon, W.B. *Yeadon's Register of LNER Locomotives Volume Two*. 2001.

Yeadon, W.B. *Yeadon's Register of LNER Locomotives Volume Three*. 2001.

Yeadon, W.B. *Yeadon's Register of LNER Locomotives Volume Four*. 2001.

Yeadon, W.B. *Yeadon's Register of LNER Locomotives Volume Six*. 2001.

Also available from Great Northern by Peter Tuffrey

The Last Days of Scottish Steam

The Last Years of Yorkshire Steam

The Golden Age of Yorkshire Railways

Gresley's A3s

Peppercorn's Pacifics

London Midland Steam 1948-1966

visit *www.greatnorthernbooks.co.uk* for details.